PESTOS SUFRITOS AND SALSAS OH MY

Must have recipes

by Michael Feeney

TABLE OF CONTENTS

PESTOS 4
- VARIATIONS 6
- SERVING SUGGESTIONS 7
- GREENS 8
- NUTS 9
- WEIGHT MANAGEMENT 11
- CLASSIC BASIL PESTO 14
- SPINACH AND WALNUT PESTO 15
- SUN-DRIED TOMATO PESTO (PESTO ROSSO) 16
- ARUGULA AND PISTACHIO PESTO 18
- CILANTRO AND PUMPKIN SEED PESTO 19
- ROASTED RED PEPPER PESTO 20
- LEMON AND BASIL PESTO 21
- SUN-DRIED TOMATO & WALNUT PESTO 22
- AVOCADO & CILANTRO PESTO 23
- ROASTED RED PEPPER & FETA PESTO 24
- SPICY JALAPEÑO & ARUGULA PESTO 25
- MORE PESTO VARIATIONS 26
- UNIQUE AND CREATIVE PESTOS 27

WHITE PESTO 30
- CLASSIC WHITE PESTO 31
- NUTTY WHITE PESTO 32
- HERBY WHITE PESTO 33

SOFRITOS 35
- CUBAN SOFRITO 39
- PUERTO RICAN SOFRITO 42
- FILIPINO SOFRITO 45
- CARIBBEAN SOFRITO 47

SALSAS 50

- CLASSIC PICO DE GALLO 51
- SALSA WITH SPICY LOVE 52
- MANGO SALSA 53
- AVOCADO SALSA 54
- SALSA 55
- CUCUMBER SALSA 56
- TROPICAL SALSA WITH A KICK 57
- MEDITERRANEAN-INSPIRED PICO DE GALLO SALSA 58

SALSA ROJAS 59

- CLASSIC MEXICAN SALSA ROJA 60
- SMOKY CHIPOTLE SALSA ROJA 61
- SALSA ROJA WITH ROASTED PEPPERS 62
- TOMATILLO-INFUSED SALSA ROJA 63
- AVOCADO AND ROASTED POBLANO SALSA VERDE 64
- KIWIFRUIT SALSA VERDE 65
- PINEAPPLE AND JALAPEÑO SALSA VERDE 66
- CUCUMBER AND BASIL SALSA VERDE 67
- GREEN APPLE AND HORSERADISH SALSA VERDE 68
- CHARRED BRUSSELS SPROUT SALSA VERDE 69

"THE SALSA THAT GOT FRUITY" 70

- CLASSIC STRAWBERRY MANGO SALSA 71
- PINEAPPLE AVOCADO SALSA 72
- WATERMELON BASIL SALSA 73
- PEACH JALAPEÑO SALSA 74
- BERRY MINT SALSA 75
- KIWI APPLE SALSA 76
- MANGO DRAGON FRUIT SALSA 77
- GRAPEFRUIT POMEGRANATE SALSA 78
- MANGO HABANERO SALSA (SWEET & FIERY) 79
- PINEAPPLE JALAPEÑO SALSA 80
- WATERMELON SERRANO SALSA 81

PESTOS

Pesto is a popular Italian sauce that is traditionally made with fresh basil, garlic, pine nuts, Parmesan or Pecorino cheese, and extra virgin olive oil. The word "pesto" comes from the Italian word "pestare," which means to pound or crush, reflecting the traditional method of preparation.

The history of pesto can be traced back to the Liguria region of northwest Italy, where it originated. The most famous variation of pesto is "Pesto alla Genovese," named after the city of Genoa in Liguria. The earliest known recipe for pesto can be found in the book "La Cuciniera Genovese," written by Giovanni Battista Ratto in 1863. This recipe closely resembles the modern Pesto alla Genovese, including basil, garlic, pine nuts, Parmesan, and olive oil.

 The use of basil as a primary ingredient is crucial to the distinct flavor of pesto. Basil has been cultivated in the Mediterranean region for centuries, and its use in Italianback to ancient times. The combination of fresh basil with other locally available ingredients contributed to the creation of pesto.

Pesto gained popularity outside of Italy in the 20th century, thanks in part to increased international travel and the global appreciation of Italian cuisine. I mean who doesn't like Italian food?   Today, pesto is enjoyed worldwide and has inspired various regional and creative adaptations. While the traditional Pesto alla Genovese remains the most well-known, you can find variations with ingredients like sun-dried tomatoes, spinach, arugula, and more.

BASIL

Fresh basil leaves are a key ingredient. The variety used is typically Genovese basil, known for its sweet and aromatic flavor.

PINE NUTS

These add a rich, nutty flavor to the pesto. They are usually toasted before being incorporated into the sauce.

GARLIC

Garlic cloves provide a pungent and savory element to the pesto. The quantity can be adjusted based on personal preference.

PARMESAN CHEESE

Aged Parmesan or Pecorino or Romano cheese is grated and added for its salty and umami-rich taste.

EXTRA VIRGIN OLIVE OIL

This is used to bind the ingredients together and create a smooth, pourable consistency.

Fresh ingredients are traditionally ground together using a mortar and pestle, hence the name "pesto."

The basil, garlic, pine nuts, and salt are gradually combined, and olive oil is added slowly to create a smooth paste.

Finally, grated cheese is stirred into the mixture.

Many people use food processors or blenders for convenience. The ingredients are still combined in the same order, with the machine saving the elbow grease.

Variations

PESTO ALLA SICILIANA

This variation includes tomatoes and almonds in addition to the traditional ingredients.

PESTO ROSSO

Also known as red pesto, it incorporates sun-dried tomatoes for a different flavor profile.

PESTO TRAPANESE

Originating from Sicily, this version includes tomatoes, almonds, and sometimes ricotta cheese.

ARUGULA PESTO

It replaces or combines basil with arugula for a peppery twist.

Kale or Spinach Pesto: These greens can be used as alternatives to basil for a milder taste.

Serving Suggestions

PASTA

Pesto is commonly tossed with pasta, creating a simple and savory dish.

Sandwiches and Wraps: It can be used as a condiment in sandwiches.

PIZZA

Pesto makes a delicious pizza sauce alternative.

VEGETABLES

It can be drizzled over roasted vegetables or used as a dip. To prevent oxidation, a thin layer of olive oil can be added

The word "pesto" comes from the Italian verb "pestare," which means to crush or grind, reflecting the traditional method of preparation. The most well-known type of pesto is Pesto. Pesto can also be frozen in ice cube trays which I highly recommend because you only have to make one batch which will have a long long long storage life especially if you empty the cubes into ziploc bags. As long as the freezer works. LOL

Pesto is a versatile sauce so it is a favorite in many kitchens around the world. Made with various herbs, nuts, and cheeses. Here are a few recipes for you to blend on!

GREENS

MINT

Mint adds a refreshing and cool flavor to pesto. It pairs well with lamb or peaTs.

ARUGULA

If you prefer a peppery kick, arugula is an excellent choice. It adds a distinct, slightly bitter flavor to the pesto.

SPINACH

For a milder flavor, spinach can be used. It's a good option if you want to increase the nutritional content of your pesto.

CILANTRO AND MINT COMBO

Combining cilantro and mint creates a unique and flavorful pesto with a hint of citrus and freshness.

DILL

Dill can be used to give your pesto a slightly tangy and aromatic quality. It pairs well with seafood. Additionally, you can customize your pesto by adding ingredients like garlic, nuts (such as pine nuts or walnuts), Parmesan or Pecorino cheese, lemon juice, and olive

OIL

Adjust the quantities based on what YOU like. Traditional pesto is made with

pine nuts, but you can experiment with different nuts to create unique flavors. Here are some nuts that work well in pesto.

NUTS

PINE NUTS

Classic pesto is made with pine nuts, which have a mild and buttery flavor.

WALNUTS

Walnuts can add a slightly bitter and earthy flavor to pesto. They are a good alternative to pine nuts and are often more budget-friendly.

ALMONDS

Almonds provide a slightly sweet and nutty flavor to pesto. You can use either raw or toasted.

PECANS

Pecans have a rich and sweet flavor, which can add a distinctive taste to your pesto.

CASHEWS

Cashews can create a creamy and milder pesto. Soaking them before blending can help achieve a smoother texture.

HAZELNUTS

add a unique, slightly sweet flavor to pesto. Toasted hazelnuts work particularly well.

MACADAMIA NUTS

Macadamia nuts have a buttery and creamy texture, making them a good choice for a rich and luxurious pesto.

Feel free to experiment and mix different nuts to find your preferred flavor combination. Additionally, you can toast the nuts before blending to enhance their flavors. Keep in mind that allergies or personal preferences may influence your choice of nuts, so consider your audience when preparing pesto.Nutrient-rich herbs: Pesto is often made with fresh basil, which is rich in vitamins A and K, as well as iron, calcium, and antioxidants. These nutrients play essential roles in maintaining various bodily functions, including bone health and immune system support.

Olive oil, a key ingredient in pesto, is a source of monounsaturated fats, which are heart-healthy. These fats may help lower bad cholesterol levels and reduce the risk of heart disease. Garlic and basil, both commonly found in pesto, contain antioxidants that help combat oxidative stress in the body. Antioxidants play a role in reducing inflammation and protecting cells from damage caused by free radicals.

Pesto often contains Parmesan or Pecorino cheese, which provides essential minerals such as calcium and phosphorus. These minerals are crucial for maintaining bone health.

Weight management

While pesto is calorie-dense due to the olive oil and cheese, the healthy fats can contribute to satiety, helping you feel full and satisfied with smaller portions. This may indirectly support weight management by reducing overall calorie intake.

Pesto is a healthy choice! Use olive oil. Here are some of the key health benefits associated with olive oil:

HEART HEALTH

Cardiovascular Benefits: Olive oil is rich in monounsaturated fats, which have been linked to a reduced risk of heart disease. It helps lower levels of LDL (bad) cholesterol and may increase levels of HDL (good) cholesterol.

Antioxidant Properties: Olive oil contains antioxidants, such as polyphenols, which help protect the lining of blood vessels and reduce inflammation, contributing to heart health.

ANTI-INFLAMMATORY EFFECTS

Olive oil has anti-inflammatory properties, which may help in reducing inflammation in the body. Chronic inflammation is associated with various diseases, including heart disease, cancer, and arthritis.

CANCER PREVENTION

Some studies suggest that the antioxidants in olive oil may have protective effects against certain types of cancer. The polyphenols in olive oil may help to neutralize free radicals, which can contribute to the development of cancer.

WEIGHT MANAGEMENT

Consuming moderate amounts of olive oil may be associated with weight management and obesity prevention. The monounsaturated fats in olive oil can contribute to a feeling of fullness, potentially reducing overall calorie intake.

BLOOD SUGAR CONTROL

Olive oil may have a positive impact on blood sugar levels and insulin sensitivity, making it beneficial for individuals with or at risk of type 2 diabetes.

BRAIN HEALTH

The monounsaturated fats and antioxidants in olive oil may contribute to brain health. Some research suggests that a Mediterranean diet, which includes olive oil, may be associated with a lower risk of cognitive decline ie." going batshit."

DIGESTIVE HEALTH

Olive oil is digestive health. It may aids in the absorption of nutrients and promotes a healthy balance of gut bacteria.

SKIN HEALTH

The antioxidants and vitamin E in olive oil may help protect the skin from damage caused by free radicals. Additionally, it is a common ingredient in skin

Classic Basil Pesto

INGREDIENTS

- 2 cups fresh basil leaves, packed
- 1/2 cup freshly grated Parmesan cheese
- 1/2 cup extra-virgin olive oil
- 1/3 cup pine nuts or walnuts
- 3 garlic cloves, peeled
- Salt and pepper to taste

INSTRUCTIONS

1. In a food processor, combine the basil, pine nuts or walnuts, and garlic. Pulse until coarsely chopped.

2. With the food processor running, gradually add the olive oil in a steady stream until the mixture is smooth.

3. Add the grated Parmesan cheese and pulse until just combined.

4. Season with salt and pepper to taste. Adjust the consistency with more olive oil if needed.

Spinach and Walnut Pesto

INGREDIENTS

▶ 3 cups fresh spinach leaves, packed

▶ 1 cup walnuts

▶ 1/2 cup grated Pecorino Romano cheese

▶ 1/2 cup extra-virgin olive oil

▶ 2 garlic cloves, peeled

▶ Salt and pepper to taste

INSTRUCTIONS:

1. In a food processor, combine the spinach, walnuts, and garlic. Pulse until coarsely chopped.

2. With the food processor running, gradually add the olive oil in a steady stream until the mixture is smooth. Add the grated Pecorino Romano cheese and pulse until just combined.

▶ cloves, peeled

▶ Fresh basil leaves (optional)

▶ Salt and pepper to taste

Sun-Dried Tomato Pesto (Pesto Rosso)

This rich and flavorful Italian pesto is perfect for pasta, sandwiches, or as a dip.

INGREDIENTS:

- 1 cup sun-dried tomatoes (packed in oil, drained, but reserve 2-3 tablespoons of the oil)
- 1/4 cup toasted pine nuts (or almonds if preferred)
- 1/4 cup grated Parmesan cheese
- 2-3 cloves garlic
- 1/2 teaspoon crushed red pepper flakes (optional, for a slight kick)
- 1/4 cup extra virgin olive oil (plus more if needed for consistency)
- 1 tablespoon balsamic vinegar
- Salt and black pepper to taste
- Fresh basil leaves (a small handful, about 5-10 leaves, optional for added freshness)

INSTRUCTIONS

1. In a food processor, combine the sun-dried tomatoes, almonds, and garlic. Pulse until coarsely chopped.

2. With the food processor running, gradually add the vinegar and then the olive oil in a steady stream until the mixture is smooth.

3. Add the grated Parmesan cheese and pulse until just combined.

Arugula and Pistachio Pesto

INGREDIENTS

- 2 cups Arugula
- 1/2 cup Pistachios
- 1/2 cup Grated Pecorino Romano cheese
- 2 garlic cloves
- 1 cup extra-virgin olive oil
- Salt and pepper to taste

INSTRUCTIONS

1. Blend arugula, pistachios, Pecorino Romano, and garlic in a food processor.
2. Gradually add olive oil until well combined.
3. Season with salt and pepper to taste.

Cilantro and Pumpkin Seed Pesto

INGREDIENTS

- 2 cups fresh cilantro
- 1/2 cups pumpkin seeds
- 1/2 cup grated Cotija cheese
- 2 garlic cloves
- 1 cup extra-virgin olive oil
- Salt and pepper to taste

INSTRUCTION

1. Blend cilantro, pumpkin seeds, Cotija cheese, and garlic in a food processor.
2. Gradually add olive oil until well combined.
3. Season with salt and pepper to taste.

Roasted Red Pepper Pesto

INGREDIENTS

- ▶ 1 cup roasted red peppers (jarred or fresh)
- ▶ ½ cup almonds
- ▶ 1 cup fresh Basil
- ▶ ½ cup grated Parmesan cheese
- ▶ 2 garlic cloves
- ▶ 1/2 cup extra-virgin olive oil
- ▶ Salt and pepper to taste

INSTRUCTIONS

1. Combine roasted red peppers, almonds, Parmesan, and garlic in a food processor.
2. Pulse until finely chopped.
3. Gradually add olive oil until smooth.
4. Season with salt and pepper to taste.

Lemon and Basil Pesto

INGREDIENTS

- 2 cups fresh basil leaves, packed
- 1/2 cup grated Parmesan cheese
- 1/3 cup pine nuts (or walnuts for a budget-friendly option)
- 2 cloves garlic, minced
- Zest of 1 lemon
- Juice of 1 lemon (about 2–3 tablespoons)
- 1/2 cup olive oil (plus more if needed)
- Salt and pepper to taste

OPTIONAL ADDITIONS

- Red pepper flakes , soy sauce.
- 2 tablespoons of fresh parsley for extra freshness

Sun-Dried Tomato & Walnut Pesto

INGREDIENTS

- ▶ 1 cup sun-dried tomatoes (packed in oil, drained)
- ▶ 1/2 cup walnuts, lightly toasted
- ▶ 1/4 cup grated Parmesan cheese
- ▶ 2 cloves garlic
- ▶ 1/3 cup olive oil
- ▶ 1/4 cup fresh basil leaves
- ▶ Salt and pepper to taste

INSTRUCTIONS

1. Combine all ingredients except the olive oil in a food processor.
2. Pulse until coarsely combined.
3. Slowly drizzle in the olive oil while blending until you achieve your desired consistency.
4. Taste and adjust seasoning.

Avocado & Cilantro Pesto

INGREDIENTS

- 1 ripe avocado
- 1/2 cup fresh cilantro leaves (packed)
- 1/4 cup almonds or pumpkin seeds
- 2 tbsp lime juice
- 1 clove garlic
- 1/4 cup olive oil
- Salt and pepper to taste

INSTRUCTIONS

1. Scoop out the avocado and add it to a blender or food processor with the cilantro, almonds, lime juice, and garlic.
2. Blend until smooth, adding olive oil gradually to reach the desired consistency.
3. Season with salt and pepper.

Roasted Red Pepper & Feta Pesto

INGREDIENTS

- ▶ 1 cup roasted red peppers (jarred or homemade)
- ▶ 1/2 cup crumbled feta cheese
- ▶ 1/3 cup pine nuts or cashews
- ▶ 2 cloves garlic
- ▶ 1/4 cup olive oil
- ▶ Salt and pepper to taste

INSTRUCTIONS

1. Blend roasted red peppers, feta, pine nuts, and garlic in a food processor until smooth.
2. Slowly add olive oil while blending.
3. Season to taste with salt and pepper.

Spicy Jalapeño & Arugula Pesto

INGREDIENTS

- 2 cups fresh arugula leaves (packed)
- 1 jalapeño (seeded for less heat, or keep seeds for extra spice)
- 1/4 cup pine nuts or pistachios
- 1/2 cup grated Parmesan cheese
- 1 clove garlic
- 1/3 cup olive oil
- Salt and pepper to taste

INSTRUCTIONS

1. In a food processor, blend arugula, jalapeño, nuts, Parmesan, and garlic until well combined.
2. Drizzle in olive oil gradually while blending until smooth.
3. Season with salt and pepper to taste.

More Pesto Variations

TRADITIONAL BASIL PESTO (PESTO ALLA GENOVESE)

Ingredients: Basil, pine nuts, garlic, Parmesan cheese, olive oil, and salt.

PARSLEY PESTO

Ingredients: Parsley, almonds or walnuts, garlic, Parmesan cheese, olive oil.

CILANTRO PESTO

Ingredients: Cilantro, lime juice, cashews or peanuts, garlic, olive oil.

SUN-DRIED TOMATO PESTO (PESTO ROSSO)

Ingredients: Sun-dried tomatoes, almonds, garlic, Parmesan, olive oil.

SPINACH PESTO

Ingredients: Spinach, walnuts, garlic, Parmesan, olive oil.

ARUGULA PESTO

Ingredients: Arugula, pecans, garlic, Parmesan, olive oil.

MINT PESTO

Ingredients: Mint leaves, almonds, lemon zest, garlic, olive oil.

Unique and Creative Pestos

KALE PESTO

Ingredients: Kale, sunflower seeds, garlic, nutritional yeast, olive oil.

BROCCOLI PESTO

Ingredients: Steamed broccoli, almonds, garlic, Parmesan, olive oil.

PISTACHIO PESTO

Ingredients: Pistachios, basil, lemon juice, garlic, Parmesan, olive oil.

AVOCADO PESTO

Ingredients: Avocado, basil, lime juice, garlic, olive oil.

BEET PESTO

Ingredients: Roasted beets, walnuts, garlic, olive oil, feta cheese (optional).

CARROT TOP PESTO

Ingredients: Carrot greens, cashews, garlic, Parmesan, olive oil.

ZUCCHINI PESTO

Ingredients: Grated zucchini, pine nuts, garlic, Parmesan, olive oil.

Another Italian cheese, Asiago, can be used in pesto to add a slightly nutty and tangy flavor.

Feel free to adjust the quantities and ingredients based on your preferences. In addition to Parmesan or Pecorino, some pesto recipes may also incorporate other types of cheeses with the exception of processed cheese. I can't in good conscience say that works for me.

It's worth noting that some people also make pesto without cheese, especially if they have dietary restrictions or preferences. In such cases, they might substitute nutritional yeast or other ingredients to achieve a similar umami flavor.

Ultimately, the choice of cheese in pesto depends on personal preference, dietary restrictions, and the desired flavor profile. So, as I always say, experiment!

Once upon a time in a small town, there was a passionate chef named Luigi who believed he had the secret to the world's best pesto sauce. He guarded his recipe like a treasure and boasted that it could make even the most stubborn taste buds swoon. He decided to enter the town's annual cooking competition, confident that his pesto would outshine all the other dishes. As he prepared his ingredients, he realized he was missing a crucial component :

pine nuts!

best thing he could find – a bag of mixed nuts, because it reminded him of his family. Luigi blended his unconventional mixture, creating a peculiar concoction that he proudly called "Nutso Pesto."

ROMANO

Similar to Parmesan and Pecorino, Romano cheese is a hard, salty cheese that can enhance the savory notes in pesto.

MANCHEGO

This Spanish cheese made from sheep's milk has a distinct flavor that can bring a unique twist to pesto.

FETA

While not traditionally Italian, feta cheese is sometimes used to create a different variation of pesto, offering a creamy and tangy taste profile.

Pesto has ancient roots, with similar sauces dating back to Roman times. The modern version, as we know it today, evolved in the Ligurian region of Italy. The use of basil in pesto became more prominent in the 19th century. The recipe gained international popularity in the 20th century as Italian cuisine that spread globally. It's most commonly associated with pasta, but it also works well as a spread, dip, or topping for pizza, sandwiches. With meat it can be used as both a marinade and as a glaze.

WHITE PESTO

White pesto, also known as pesto bianco, is a variation of the traditional green pesto sauce that typically contains basil, garlic, pine nuts, Parmesan cheese, and olive oil. The main difference is the absence of fresh basil, which gives it a lighter color and a milder, nuttier flavor. White pesto may include a variety of ingredients, and recipes can vary, but common components include:

Garlic: A key ingredient for flavoring the pesto.

Nuts: Instead of pine nuts, almonds, cashews, or walnuts are often used in white pesto.

Cheese: Parmesan or Pecorino Romano cheese is commonly used, providing a salty and savory element.

Olive Oil: Like traditional pesto, white pesto relies on high-quality olive oil for its smooth consistency and rich taste.

Herbs: While the basil is omitted, other herbs like parsley, mint, or cilantro may be included to add freshness and depth.

Lemon Juice: Some recipes incorporate lemon juice to brighten the flavor and add a citrusy kick.

Salt and Pepper: Used to season the pesto to taste.

Optional Ingredients: Depending on the recipe, other ingredients such as grated pecorino, ricotta, or even cream may be added to enhance creaminess.

Classic White Pesto

(Ricotta and Parmesan-Based)

INGREDIENTS

- 1 cup ricotta cheese
- 1/2 cup grated Parmesan cheese
- 1/4 cup pine nuts (lightly toasted)
- 2 garlic cloves (minced)
- 1/4 cup olive oil
- Zest and juice of 1 lemon
- Salt and pepper to taste

INSTRUCTIONS

1. Combine the ricotta, Parmesan, pine nuts, and garlic in a food processor. Blend until smooth.
2. Slowly drizzle in olive oil while blending until the mixture is creamy.
3. Add lemon juice and zest, then season with salt and pepper. Blend briefly to mix.
4. Serve over pasta, as a dip, or a spread on bread.

Nutty White Pesto

(Cashew and Cream-Based)

INGREDIENTS

- 1 cup raw cashews (soaked in water for 2 hours, then drained)
- 1/2 cup grated Pecorino cheese
- 1/2 cup heavy cream or Greek yogurt
- 2 garlic cloves
- 1/4 cup olive oil
- Salt and pepper to taste

INSTRUCTIONS

1. Add the cashews, Pecorino, and garlic to a food processor. Blend until finely chopped.
2. Add the cream (or yogurt) and blend until smooth.
3. Drizzle in olive oil and season with salt and pepper. Adjust creaminess by adding more cream or olive oil if desired.
4. Toss with roasted vegetables, spread on sandwiches, or use as a pizza base.

Herby White Pesto

(Basil and Almond-Based)

INGREDIENTS:

- 1 cup blanched almonds
- 1/2 cup grated Parmesan cheese
- 1/2 cup fresh basil leaves
- 1/4 cup fresh parsley or arugula
- 2 garlic cloves
- 1/4 cup olive oil
- 1/4 cup cream cheese or mascarpone
- Salt and pepper to taste

INSTRUCTIONS:

1. Pulse the almonds, Parmesan, basil, parsley (or arugula), and garlic in a food processor until coarse.

2. Add the cream cheese (or mascarpone) and blend until smooth.

3. Drizzle in olive oil and season with salt (optional)

WHITE PESTO PASTA

Cook your favorite pasta according to package instructions.

In a blender or food processor, combine garlic, almonds, Parmesan cheese, olive oil, and any chosen herbs.

Blend until smooth, adding salt, pepper, and lemon juice to taste.

Toss the cooked pasta with the white pesto sauce until well coated.

WHITE PESTO PIZZA

Spread a thin layer of white pesto on pizza dough.

Top with ingredients like mozzarella, cherry tomatoes, and prosciutto.

Bake until the crust is golden and the cheese is melted.

WHITE PESTO CHICKEN SALAD

Mix shredded cooked chicken with white pesto.

Add cherry tomatoes, arugula, and any other desired salad ingredients.

Toss until everything is coated in the pesto and serve.

SOFRITOS

A sofrito is a flavorful base used in many Latin American and Mediterranean cuisines. It's a mixture of aromatic ingredients that are finely chopped, sautéed, and used as a foundation for the be dishes. The specific ingredients can vary by region, but common components include onions, garlic, bell peppers, tomatoes, and herbs. Now obviously these ingredients can turn into a thin pesto like sauce with the help of the trusty food processor to the consistency that works for you.

Latin American SofritoSofrito is a flavorful base used in many Latin American and Caribbean cuisines, characterized by its blend of aromatic ingredients that add depth and complexity to a wide variety of dishes. While its composition varies by region and personal preference, sofrito typically includes a mix of vegetables, herbs, and spices. Here's an overview:

PREPARATION

Sofrito can be made fresh or in bulk and frozen for convenience. Many families have their own unique recipe, handed down through generations.

Would you like a specific recipe or more details about a particular type of sofrito?

Sofrito is a flavorful base used in many Latin American and Caribbean cuisines, characterized by its blend of aromatic ingredients that add depth and complexity to a wide variety of dishes. While its composition varies by region and personal preference, sofrito typically includes a mix of vegetables, herbs,

and spices. Here's an overview:

COMMON INGREDIENTS

Onions: Provide a sweet, savory base.

Garlic: Adds pungency and depth.

Bell Peppers: Often green or red, they add sweetness and color.

Tomatoes: Frequently included, especially in Caribbean and South American variations.

Cilantro: A fresh, herbal note, commonly used in Puerto Rican and Dominican sofrito.

Culantro: A stronger herb often found in Caribbean varieties.

Spices: Cumin, oregano, and paprika are popular additions.

Chilies: Some versions include mild or hot chilies for heat.

REGIONAL VARIATIONS

Puerto Rican Sofrito: Features culantro (recao), sweet peppers (ají dulce), and often a mix of green ingredients. It's typically blended or finely chopped.

Dominican Sofrito (Sazón): Similar to Puerto Rican sofrito but may include vinegar or sour orange for a tangy touch.

Cuban Sofrito: Leans heavily on onions, garlic, and bell peppers, with tomatoes playing a significant role.

Mexican Sofrito: Often cooked and includes tomatoes, garlic, onions, and chili peppers, forming the base for salsas and stews.

South American Sofrito: In countries like Colombia and Venezuela, it might include achiote (annatto) for color and is often sautéed in oil.

Catalonia: May include additional garlic or nuts like almonds.

Andalusia: Sometimes leans on bell peppers and omits tomatoes.

Caribbean Sofrito: A related but distinct version popular in Puerto Rican or Cuban cuisine, featuring cilantro, culantro, and other tropical herbs.

HOW IT'S USED

Sofrito is typically sautéed in oil before other ingredients are added, creating a rich base for dishes like:

Rice (e.g., arroz con gandules or arroz con pollo)

Soups and stews (e.g., sancocho, picadillo)

Beans

Meats and seafood dishes

INGREDIENTS:

Onions, garlic, tomatoes, and bell peppers are the core components.

Sometimes, it might include paprika for a smoky flavor. It's commonly used in Spanish paella, sauces, and stews.

Italian Soffritto Italian soffritto (not to be confused with Spanish sofrito) is a foundational element in Italian cuisine. It typically consists of a finely chopped mixture of aromatic vegetables, usually onion, celery, and carrot (known as the "holy trinity").

FUN FACT

The practice of using a mixture of aromatic vegetables as a flavor base is widespread in many cuisines:

The French have mirepoix (onion, celery, and carrot, often cooked in butter).

The Spanish sofrito typically includes tomatoes and peppers in addition to onion and garlic.

Cuban Sofrito

INGREDIENTS:

- 2 tablespoons olive oil
- 1 medium yellow onion, finely diced
- 1 medium green bell pepper, finely diced
- 4-5 cloves garlic, minced
- 1-2 Roma tomatoes, finely chopped or grated (optional)
- 2 teaspoons ground cumin
- 1 teaspoon dried oregano
- 1/2 teaspoon smoked paprika (optional but adds depth)
- 1-2 tablespoons tomato paste (optional for richness)
- Salt and pepper, to taste
- Fresh cilantro, finely chopped (optional for garnish)

INSTRUCTIONS:

1. **Heat the Oil:** Heat the olive oil in a large skillet or saucepan over medium heat.

2. **Sauté Onions and Peppers:** Add the diced onion and green bell pepper to the skillet. Cook for 4-5 minutes, stirring occasionally, until softened and

translucent.

3. **Add Garlic:** Stir in the minced garlic and cook for about 30 seconds to 1 minute, until fragrant.

4. **Incorporate Tomatoes (if using):** Add the chopped or grated tomatoes. Cook for another 3-4 minutes, stirring frequently, until the tomatoes break down and integrate with the mixture.: Sprinkle in the cumin, oregano, smoked paprika (if using), and a pinch of salt and pepper. Mix well to coat the vegetables in the spices. Stir in the tomato paste if you want a richer base. Cook for another 1-2 minutes, allowing the flavors to meld. Taste and adjust seasoning if needed. If using cilantro, stir it in or use it as a garnish when the sofrito is added to a dish.

USES IN CUBAN CUISINE

Rice dishes: Like arroz con pollo (chicken with rice) or congri (rice and beans).

Soups and stews: Such as ropa vieja (shredded beef) and picadillo (ground beef hash).

Bean dishes: Including black beans, which are a Cuban staple.

Cuban sofrito is distinct from its counterparts in other cuisines, like Puerto Rican or Spanish sofrito.

For example:

Cuban sofrito tends to be simpler and uses fewer herbs, focusing on garlic, onions, and peppers.

Puerto Rican sofrito might include culantro, aji dulce (sweet peppers), and recao, making it more herbaceous.

Onions, garlic, bell peppers, and tomatoes are standard, with additional elements like cumin and oregano for a distinct Cuban flavor. It's a fundamental component in

Cuban cuisine, often used in rice and bean dishes like Moros y Cristianos.

Puerto Rican Sofrito Spanish sofrito is a foundational ingredient in many Spanish dishes, serving as a flavor base similar to the French mirepoix or Italian soffritto. It is made by gently cooking finely chopped vegetables, typically in olive oil, until they become soft and aromatic. Here's a closer look:

Puerto Rican Sofrito

INGREDIENTS

- ▶ 1 large green bell pepper, seeded and chopped
- ▶ 1 large red bell pepper, seeded and chopped
- ▶ 1 medium onion, chopped
- ▶ 1 head of garlic, peeled
- ▶ 1 bunch of cilantro, rinsed and roughly chopped
- ▶ 1 small bunch of culantro (recao), rinsed and roughly chopped (optional but authentic)
- ▶ 4-5 ajíes dulces (small sweet peppers), seeded and chopped (optional, adds authentic flavor)
- ▶ 1 large tomato, chopped (optional)
- ▶ 2-3 tablespoons olive oil (optional, for texture and preservation)

INSTRUCTIONS

Prepare the Ingredients: Wash all vegetables and herbs thoroughly. Chop them into smaller pieces for easier blending.

BLEND OR PROCESS:

- ▶ Add all ingredients into a blender or food processor.

▶ Pulse or blend until you get a coarse or smooth consistency, depending on your preference. Avoid making it too watery.

OPTIONAL ADDITIONS

Paprika (pimentón): Sweet or smoky, it enhances the depth of flavor.

Bay leaves: Adds a subtle aromatic touch.

Herbs: Such as thyme, oregano, or parsley.

Wine: Red or white wine can sometimes be added to deglaze the pan and boost flavor.

PREPARATION

1. Chop the vegetables finely to ensure even cooking and a uniform texture.
2. Heat olive oil in a pan over medium heat.
3. Cook the onion first, allowing it to soften and turn translucent.
4. Add garlic and bell peppers, cooking gently to release their flavors.
5. Stir in the tomatoes, letting them break down and meld with the other ingredients.
6. Simmer until the mixture has reduced slightly and has a rich, cohesive texture.

USES

Sofrito is versatile and appears in many traditional Spanish dishes, such as:

Paella: It serves as the aromatic base for the iconic rice dish.

Stews: Adds depth to meat and vegetable stews.

SOUPS AND SAUCES

Culantro (recao), bell peppers, onions, garlic, tomatoes, and sometimes aji dulce peppers. It's a key ingredient in Puerto Rican cuisine, used in dishes like arroz con gandules (rice with pigeon peas) and stews.

Filipino Sofrito is a flavorful seasoning base used in Filipino cuisine to enhance dishes, particularly in stews, soups, and rice-based recipes. It is inspired by the sofrito found in Spanish and Latin American cooking, reflecting the Philippines' colonial history and the fusion of culinary traditions.

Filipino Sofrito

(Ginisang Bawang)

INGREDIENTS

- 3 tablespoons cooking oil (vegetable, canola, or coconut oil)
- 6 cloves garlic, minced
- 1 medium onion, diced
- 3 medium tomatoes, diced
- 1 teaspoon fish sauce (optional, for an authentic Filipino touch)
- 1/4 teaspoon ground black pepper and salt

INSTRUCTIONS

1. **Heat the oil:** In a large skillet or pan, heat the cooking oil over medium heat.
2. **Sauté the garlic:** Add the minced garlic and sauté until fragrant and lightly golden (about 1 minute).
3. **Add the onions:** Stir in the diced onions and cook until they become translucent (about 2-3 minutes).
4. **Cook the tomatoes:** Add the diced tomatoes and mash them slightly with a spoon or spatula.
5. Cook until the tomatoes break down and release their juices, creating a

slightly chunky sauce (about 5-7 minutes).

6. **Season:** Add fish sauce (if using), ground black pepper, and a pinch of salt. Adjust seasoning to taste.

7. **Cool or use immediately:** Your Filipino sofrito is now ready! You can use it as a base for dishes like adobo, sinigang, menudo, or pansit, or store it in an airtight container in the fridge for up to a week.

To add more depth of flavor, you can include a small amount of crushed ginger or finely chopped bell peppers. For a spicier version, throw in some chopped siling labuyo (bird's eye chili) or chili flakes. This sofrito can also be blended for a smoother consistency if desired.

Caribbean Sofrito

INGREDITENTS

- 1 medium onion (roughly chopped)
- 1 bell pepper (green, red, or a mix, roughly chopped)
- 4-6 cloves of garlic
- 1 cup cilantro (including stems, roughly chopped)
- 1 cup culantro (recao) (if available, roughly chopped; substitute with more cilantro if unavailable)
- 4-6 ají dulce (sweet peppers) (seeded, optional but authentic)
- 2 scallions (green onions) (roughly chopped)
- 1 small tomato (optional, roughly chopped)
- 1 tablespoon fresh oregano (or 1 teaspoon dried oregano)
- 1 teaspoon salt (adjust to taste)
- 1 teaspoon ground black pepper
- 2-3 tablespoons olive oil
- 1 tablespoon vinegar or lime juice (optional, for brightness)

INSTRUCTIONS

1. **Prepare Ingredients:** Wash and roughly chop all vegetables and herbs to

make blending easier.

2. **Blend or Process:** Add all ingredients to a food processor or blender. Pulse until you achieve your desired consistency. Some prefer it chunky, while others like it smooth.

3. **Taste and Adjust:** Check for seasoning and adjust salt, pepper, or lime juice as needed.

4. **Store:** Transfer to a glass jar or airtight container. Refrigerate for up to 1 week or freeze in ice cube trays for longer storage.

IN ADOBO VARIATIONS (THOUGH NOT ALL USE SOFRITO)

▶ Menudo

▶ Afritada

▶ Arroz Valenciana

▶ Soups like sinigang or pochero

▶ Fried rice dishes

Pestos and Soffrito use similar ingredients but provide different flavor profiles. As always, dear reader, I recommend experimenting with the ingredients and their quantities to get what you like most and make it your own.

If regular salsa is the life of the party, fruit salsa is the one who shows up wearing a Hawaiian shirt and passing out sunglasses.

Bursting with juicy berries, tangy citrus, and a little kick of lime, fruit salsa is the sweet, sassy cousin of your classic dip. It's the perfect excuse to eat a whole bowl of fruit while pretending you're being healthy (we won't tell if you pair it with a mountain of cinnamon chips). Whether you're jazzing up tacos, topping off grilled fish, or just eating it by the spoonful, fruit salsa is here to turn snack time into a fiesta!

Salsas

Salsas who doesn't love them? There are many kinds and you can put them on everything even on ice cream! They are a versatile and flavorful sauce or condiment originating from Latin American cuisine, known for its vibrant and fresh ingredients. It typically combines tomatoes, chili peppers, onions, cilantro, lime juice, and salt, though variations abound. Salsas can be categorized by their texture (chunky or smooth), temperature (fresh or cooked), and spice level. Popular types include:

Pico de Gallo: A fresh, chunky salsa made with raw ingredients.

Salsa Roja: A red, cooked salsa often made with roasted tomatoes and peppers.

Salsa Verde: A green salsa featuring tomatillos and green chilies.

Fruit Salsas: Sweet and tangy, incorporating fruits like mango or pineapple.

Salsas are commonly used as dips, toppings for tacos, or accompaniments for grilled meats and other dishes. Their adaptability makes them a staple in many cuisines. What follows is the basics to the unusual in that order for these culinary accoutrements.

Classic Pico de Gallo

INGREDIENTS

- 4 Roma tomatoes, diced
- 1 medium white onion, finely chopped
- 1-2 jalapeños, minced (adjust for spice level)
- 1/4 cup fresh cilantro, chopped
- Juice of 1 lime
- Salt to taste

INSTRUCTIONS

1. Combine ingredients and chill for 1 hour before serving.

Salsa with Spicy Love

INGREDIENTS:

- 4 tomatoes, diced
- 1 small red onion, finely chopped
- 2 serrano peppers, finely chopped
- 1 yellow or red Bell Pepper finely chopped
- ½ cup cilantro, chopped
- Juice of 1 lime with the zest
- 1/2 tsp cayenne pepper
- ½ tsp Salt
- ½ tsp fresh ground black pepper

INSTRUCTIONS

1. Mix all ingredients in a bowl. Let rest for 20 minutes before serving to intensify heat.

MANGO SALSA

INGREDIENTS

- 2 tomatoes, diced
- 1 cup diced mango
- ½ cup seedless grapes halved
- 1 small Bermuda (red) onion, chopped
- 1 jalapeño, finely chopped
- 1/4 cup fresh mint, chopped
- 1 Tbsp lemon juice

INSTRUCTIONS

1. Combine all ingredients and give them an hour to meld flavors

Avocado Salsa

INGREDIENTS

▶ 3 Roma tomatoes, diced

▶ 1 small Vidalia onion, chopped

▶ 1 avocado, diced

▶ 1 jalapeño, minced

▶ 1/4 cup Basil, chopped

▶ Juice of 1 lemon

▶ Salt to taste

INSTRUCTIONS

1. Gently combine all ingredients in a bowl. Serve immediately to avoid avocado browning.

Salsa

INGREDIENTS:

- 2 cups cooked corn kernels
- 2 tomatoes, diced
- 1 Green Bell Pepper diced
- 1 small Bermuda (red) onion, chopped
- 1 jalapeño, minced
- 1/4 cup Parsley and Cilantro chopped and combined
- 1 Tbsp of lemon juice
- 2 Tbsp extra virgin olive oil
- 1 Tbsp of tri colored fresh ground pepper and a pinch of salt (optional)

INSTRUCTIONS

1. Combine and chill before serving with a corny joke.

Cucumber Salsa

INGREDIENTS:

- 3 tomatoes, diced
- 1 cup cucumber, diced
- ½ cup diced Bermuda Onion
- 1 jalapeño, minced
- 1/4 cup Basil, chopped
- 1 tsp lime juice
- 2 Tbsp of Italian Dressing

INSTRUCTIONS

1. Mix and chill before serving

Tropical Salsa with a Kick

INGREDIENTS

- 2 ripe mangoes, diced
- 1 cup diced fresh pineapple
- 2 medium tomatoes, diced
- 1 red bell pepper, diced
- 1 small red onion, finely chopped
- 1 Serrano pepper, finely chopped (adjust for heat)
- 2 tablespoons fresh cilantro, chopped
- Juice of 1 lime
- Zest of 1 lime
- 1 teaspoon chili powder
- 1 teaspoon honey (optional, for added sweetness)
- Pinch of salt

INSTRUCTIONS

1. Combine all ingredients in a large bowl.

Mediterranean-Inspired Pico de Gallo Salsa

INGREDIENTS

- 2 medium tomatoes, diced
- 1 cucumber, diced
- 1/2 cup kalamata olives, chopped
- 1/2 cup crumbled feta cheese
- 1 small red onion, finely chopped
- 1 clove garlic, minced
- 1 tablespoon capers, rinsed and chopped
- 1 tablespoon fresh dill, chopped
- Juice of 1 lemon
- 3 tablespoons extra-virgin olive oil
- 1 teaspoon dried oregano
- Pinch of black pepper

INSTRUCTIONS

1. In a large bowl, combine the tomatoes, cucumber, olives, red onion, and capers.

2. Add feta, dill, garlic, oregano, and black pepper. Drizzle olive oil and lemon juice.

Salsa Rojas

Salsa Roja, meaning "red sauce" in Spanish, is a vibrant and flavorful Mexican condiment typically made from a blend of red tomatoes, chili peppers, onions, garlic, and spices. It's a cornerstone of Mexican cuisine, known for its bold, smoky, and slightly spicy flavor profile.

Salsa Roja can vary in heat level depending on the type and amount of chili peppers used, such as jalapeños, serranos, or guajillos. It can be made with raw or roasted ingredients, the latter giving it a deeper and smokier taste. The ingredients are often blended or finely chopped and cooked to enhance their flavors.

This versatile sauce is used in countless dishes, including tacos, enchiladas, tamales, and as a dip for tortilla chips. Its fresh, tangy, and spicy qualities make it a favorite for adding a burst of flavor to meals.

Classic Mexican Salsa Roja

INGREDIENTS:

▶ 4 Roma tomatoes

▶ 2 cloves garlic

▶ 1 small white onion (quartered)

▶ 2-3 dried guajillo chiles

▶ 1 dried ancho chile

▶ Salt to taste

INSTRUCTIONS

1. Toast the chiles lightly on a skillet until fragrant. Remove seeds and stems.

2. Boil the tomatoes, onion, garlic, and toasted chiles in water until the tomatoes soften (about 10 minutes).

3. Blend everything until smooth, adding a bit of the boiling water if needed for consistency.

4. Season with salt and serve warm or cold.

Smoky Chipotle Salsa Roja

INGREDIENTS:

- 3 large tomatoes
- 2 canned chipotle peppers in adobo
- 1 clove garlic
- 1 small red onion (diced)
- 1 tbsp olive oil
- Salt and pepper to taste

INSTRUCTIONS:

1. Roast the tomatoes and garlic on a dry skillet or grill until charred.
2. Blend the roasted ingredients with chipotle peppers until smooth.
3. Heat olive oil in a pan, add the blended salsa, and cook for 5-7 minutes. Season with salt and pepper.

Salsa Roja with Roasted Peppers

INGREDIENTS

▶ 4 Roma tomatoes

▶ 1 red bell pepper (roasted and peeled)

▶ 1 serrano chile (optional for heat)

▶ 2 cloves garlic

▶ ½ cup cilantro

▶ Salt and lime juice to taste

INSTRUCTIONS

1. Roast the tomatoes and serrano chile until slightly charred.

2. Blend the roasted tomatoes, bell pepper, chile, garlic, and cilantro until smooth.

3. Add lime juice and salt to taste.

Tomatillo-Infused Salsa Roja

INGREDIENTS

- 3 tomatoes
- 2 tomatillos
- 2 dried árbol chiles
- 1 clove garlic
- 1 tsp cumin
- Salt to taste

INSTRUCTIONS

1. Roast the tomatoes and tomatillos on a skillet. Toast the árbol chiles lightly. Blend all the ingredients together, including garlic, cumin, and salt. Add water for desired consistency.
2. Serve fresh with tortilla chips or tacos.

SALSA VERDES

Avocado and Roasted Poblano Salsa Verde

INGREDIENTS

- 2 roasted poblano peppers
- 2 ripe avocados
- 3 tomatillos, husked and roasted
- 1 clove garlic
- Juice of 1 lime
- 1/2 cup cilantro leaves
- 1/4 teaspoon cumin
- Salt to taste

INSTRUCTIONS

1. Blend all the ingredients until smooth for a creamy and smoky twist on traditional salsa verde.

Kiwifruit Salsa Verde

INGREDIENTS

- 4 ripe kiwis, peeled and diced
- 2 tomatillos, raw and diced
- 1 green chili (like serrano or jalapeño), finely chopped
- 1/4 cup cilantro leaves, chopped
- Juice of 1 lime
- Salt and pepper to taste

INSTRUCTIONS

1. Combine all ingredients in a bowl, mixing gently. Serve fresh with grilled fish or chicken.

Pineapple and Jalapeño Salsa Verde

INGREDIENTS

- 1 cup fresh pineapple, diced
- 3 roasted tomatillos
- 1 jalapeño, roasted and chopped
- 1/4 cup fresh mint leaves
- Juice of 1/2 lemon
- Salt to taste

INSTRUCTIONS

1. Blend pineapple, tomatillos, and jalapeño for a tropical, zesty salsa. Add mint and lemon juice, then pulse briefly.

Cucumber and Basil Salsa Verde

INGREDIENTS:

- 1 cucumber, peeled and diced
- 3 tomatillos, roasted
- 1 green chili, chopped
- 1/4 cup fresh basil leaves
- 1 tablespoon olive oil
- Salt and black pepper to taste

INSTRUCTIONS

1. Blend tomatillos, chili, and cucumber until smooth. Stir in olive oil, basil, salt, and pepper.

Green Apple and Horseradish Salsa Verde

INGREDIENTS

- 1 green apple, peeled and diced
- 2 tomatillos, roasted
- 1 teaspoon fresh grated horseradish
- 1/4 cup parsley leaves
- 1/4 cup cilantro leaves
- Juice of 1 lime
- Salt to taste

INSTRUCTIONS

1. Blend all ingredients into a tangy and sharp salsa perfect for pairing with roast pork.

Charred Brussels Sprout Salsa Verde

INGREDIENTS

- 1 cup Brussels sprouts, charred and chopped
- 2 roasted tomatillos
- 1 green chili, chopped
- 1 clove garlic
- 2 tablespoons apple cider vinegar
- 1/4 cup cilantro
- Salt and pepper to taste

INSTRUCTIONS

1. Blend roasted tomatillos, garlic, and chili. Stir in chopped Brussels sprouts, vinegar, cilantro, salt, and pepper for a smoky and earthy salsa verde.

"The Salsa That Got Fruity"

Move over, tomatoes—this salsa just got a tropical makeover! Bursting with juicy mangoes, zesty pineapples, and just enough spice to make them interesting. fruit salsa isn't here to be subtle. It's the life of the party, the ultimate wingman for your tortilla chips. Get ready to pucker, crunch, and savor every sweet and spicy bite! Some salsas play it safe—mild, predictable, and all about the tomatoes. These salsas hit the dance floor with a pineapple under one arm and a mango under the other, spinning into a whirlwind of sweet and spicy. It's bold, it's colorful, and it's definitely the most popular bowl at the party.

Just don't blame me if your chips start fighting over it.

Classic Strawberry Mango Salsa

INGREDIENTS

- 1 cup diced strawberries
- 1 cup diced mango
- ½ cup diced red bell pepper
- ¼ cup finely chopped red onion
- 1 jalapeño, minced
- Juice of 1 lime
- ¼ cup chopped cilantro
- Salt to taste

DIRECTIONS

1. Mix all ingredients in a bowl, chill for 15 minutes, and serve.

Pineapple Avocado Salsa

INGREDIENTS

▶ 1 cup diced pineapple

▶ 1 diced avocado

▶ ¼ cup chopped red onion

▶ 1 jalapeño, minced

▶ Juice of 1 lime

▶ ¼ cup chopped cilantro

▶ Salt to taste

DIRECTIONS

1. Gently mix all ingredients, chill, and enjoy.

Watermelon Basil Salsa

INGREDIENTS

- 1 ½ cups diced watermelon
- ½ cup diced cucumber
- ¼ cup chopped fresh basil
- Juice of 1 lime
- ½ tsp honey
- Salt and pepper to taste

DIRECTIONS

1. Combine all ingredients, mix well, and serve chilled.

Peach Jalapeño Salsa

INGREDIENTS

- 2 ripe peaches, diced
- ½ cup diced red bell pepper
- 1 small jalapeño, minced
- ¼ cup diced red onion
- Juice of 1 lime
- ¼ cup chopped cilantro
- Salt to taste

DIRECTIONS

1. Mix everything in a bowl and chill before serving.

Berry Mint Salsa

INGREDIENTS

- ½ cup diced strawberries
- ½ cup diced blueberries
- ½ cup diced raspberries
- 1 tbsp chopped fresh mint
- 1 tbsp honey
- Juice of ½ lemon

DIRECTIONS

1. Toss ingredients together and serve with cinnamon chips.

Kiwi Apple Salsa

INGREDIENTS

- 2 kiwis, diced
- 1 small green apple, diced
- ½ cup diced cucumber
- Juice of 1 lime
- 1 tbsp honey
- ¼ cup chopped cilantro

DIRECTIONS

1. Combine all ingredients and let sit for 10 minutes before serving.

Mango Dragon Fruit Salsa

INGREDIENTS

- 1 cup diced mango
- 1 cup diced dragon fruit
- ¼ cup finely chopped red onion
- Juice of 1 lime
- 1 tbsp honey
- ¼ cup chopped mint or cilantro

DIRECTIONS

1. Mix everything and chill for 20 minutes.

Grapefruit Pomegranate Salsa

INGREDIENTS

- 1 grapefruit, peeled and diced
- ½ cup pomegranate seeds
- ¼ cup chopped green onion
- 1 tbsp honey
- Juice of 1 lemon

DIRECTIONS

1. Gently mix all ingredients and serve chilled.

Mango Habanero Salsa (Sweet & Fiery)

INGREDIENTS

- 2 ripe mangoes, diced
- 1 small red onion, finely chopped
- 1 red bell pepper, diced
- 1-2 habanero peppers, minced (adjust to taste)
- Juice of 2 limes
- 1/4 cup fresh cilantro, chopped
- Salt to taste

Instructions

1. Combine all ingredients in a bowl.
2. Mix well and taste for spice and salt.
3. Chill for 20 minutes before serving.
4. **Pairs well with:** Grilled chicken, fish tacos, or tortilla chips.

Pineapple Jalapeño Salsa

(Tropical & Zesty)

INGREDIENTS

- 2 cups fresh pineapple, diced
- 1 large jalapeño, seeded and minced
- 1 small red onion, finely chopped
- 1/2 cup cherry tomatoes, quartered
- Juice of 1 lemon
- 1 tablespoon honey
- 1/4 cup fresh mint, chopped
- Salt and pepper to taste

INSTRUCTIONS

1. Mix all ingredients in a bowl.
2. Adjust sweetness and seasoning as needed.
3. Serve immediately or refrigerate.
4. Pairs well with: Grilled shrimp, pork chops, or nachos.

Watermelon Serrano Salsa

(Refreshing & Bold)

INGREDIENTS

- 3 cups seedless watermelon, diced
- 1 serrano pepper, minced
- 1/2 cup cucumber, diced
- 1/4 cup red onion, finely chopped
- Juice of 1 lime
- 1 tablespoon rice vinegar
- 1/4 cup fresh basil, chopped
- Salt to taste

INSTRUCTIONS

1. Gently toss all ingredients together.
2. Let sit for 10 minutes to blend flavors.
3. Serve chilled.
4. **Pairs well with:** Grilled salmon, tacos al pastor, or as a salad topping

Well dear reader that is all I have for you now and I hope you enjoy some of the ideas. Remember to stick with no plan and just have fun when creating your own dishes.

Ciao!! Till the next time.

Mike F